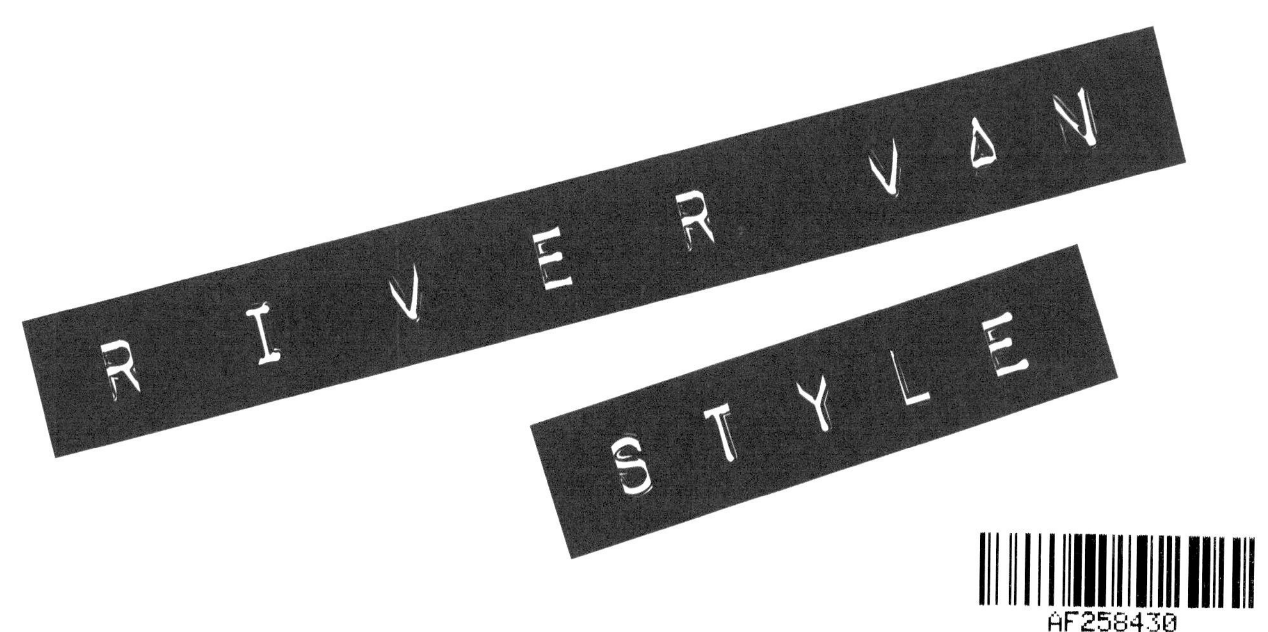

Vol. 1 - Gross Restore

Publisher: F. Mika Guerrehors
Editor: Clive Eno

2019
London

Vol. 1
Gross Restore
Send us your work:
SUBMISSIONS@RIVERVANSTYLE.COM | WWW.RIVERVANSTYLE.COM

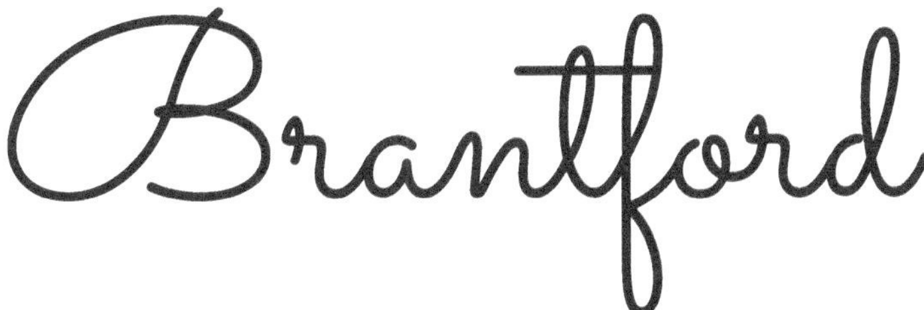

Fiction

FLASH

Sunday Roast: I loved someone permanently stuck in this song, as dictated by *her* girlfriend, a young woman at the time. Their love/hate relationship had a little run-off into my shipyard, but for me the line "I know all your stories but I'll listen to them again." didn't quite fit because I haven't repeated any stories. Unless I'm stuck there in the co-pilot deck - being there, socially, speaking, requires exaggerated alcohol intake. Does she know who I am?

I've heard her stories a few

times. Is the alcohol speaking

directly to me? I've noticed this

most of all

the people who care, and noticed this when I care: those individuals who enter my life, who become real, unique individuals are the true friends I've sought.

On A Clear Day

Michael Whone

At the end of February I was at the hospital to have a monthly Paliperidone injection for schizo-affective disorder. The doctor discusses with me how I'm doing and how my daily life is treating me. He asks me if I am sleeping well, or if I have taken any street drugs or alcohol. He asks me if I hear and see things that aren't there. Does he mean people I hear on the phone?—actors in movies? Our lonely existence is built on the entertainment of gladly being schizoid—carrying out nearly every relationship absent of tangibility. I've tried to invest my heart and soul into people, have never seen a return on investment, and it's deteriorating of self. Everything I say to the doctor is a façade and if I was to say how I truly felt sometimes, I could get locked up in the psych ward of the hospital. In actuality, everyone has the same problems as me, but the ninety-five percent of people without schizophrenic disorders are generally a little more steadfast for the better parts of their lifetimes.

The last time I was there, before today, I was late and the nurse that injects me called me on the phone when I was at the college library having a text message conversation with my sister. My sister was telling me about all the skills I have and the potential I have to start teaching music again. She moved me to tears, or was it an electronic device that moved me?—no one was actually there. There were people in the library, but they were unapproachable, unlikely to be intertwined with my path. I didn't want to go see the nurse, or the doctor. I felt good conversing with my sister.

There was a time in my life when I was rude and unpleasant toward my sister, she was rude and unpleasant to me, and our malice toward each became rampant among us. These days, my sister says that in some dimension or realm, our entities chose to deliver the two of us, intertwined in our earthly bodies, to experience life in meaningful acquaintance. Therein is the bond which defies the modern disconnect—which defies the schizoidia. It only takes one chapter, one line, or one gesture to feel arable in the Februaries of life. Other than my connection with her, I've always wondered if there could be someone other than her to partake with. A few years ago, in Japan, the terminology for schizophrenia changed from a term meaning *mind-split-disease* to a term meaning *integration disorder*. After receiving my diagnosis of schizo-affective, I began realizing that for my entire life the symptoms had been there and the resultant depths I fell into lead me to leaving musicianship behind, only to develop the belief that the other ninety-five percent suddenly became schizoid.

I told the nurse that I couldn't go to the hospital that day. She seemed upset, and now, a month later, I look back on it and accept that she was right to be upset with me. Degeneration of personality is common among schizophrenics, so disassociation from her, my most frequent point of human contact, could pose as a threat to my future.

No matter, my conversation with my sister ended and I left the library. As I walked the halls of the college, I saw two paramedics with a stretcher walking through the main entrance. They were probably students but I had a vivid mental image of the times I had been locked in mental institutions being forced to take drugs for any and every problem I might have accidentally mentioned to the nurses and doctors. Believe me: you should be honest only in moderation. In fighting any onset of psychosis and the fright that I might be locked up again, I quickly made my way to the hospital, ill-equipped for the night ahead.

I *had been* feeling great overall. I had just met a new woman at the college and I was friends with a self-proclaimed Indian guru who sometimes entertained me while doing mundane errands. It was a Tuesday night when I was grocery shopping with my best buddy, the dishwasher, who moved here from Punjab. He described his leaving Punjab as a kind of *actual* escapism, rather than the kind you get watching television. So, he made a connection with me the day he arrived in Canada for freedom.

As he compared prices of chicken breasts, in the back of my mind I was thinking that Valentine's Day was on Friday. Then Vishal went to check out with his groceries and I noticed a bin that had Valentine's cards for three dollars. Vishal was charming the young female cashier with his thick Punjabi accent when I chimed in to ask her for a dose of perspicacity. I asked if she thought it would be strange if I bought some Valentines and handed them out at the college on Friday. "I think that would be cute, no one does that anymore," she said. Her timely sagacity was convincing enough that I bought the cards with my last five dollars. I procrastinated writing my name on the cards until Thursday night.

On Friday morning at the college café, a blonde and brunette sat at the table next to me having a conversation. I didn't have enough courage to give them the cards. I walked through the halls, almost defeated, and went outside to have a cigarette. Not much later, that same brunette was outside smoking right beside me, so I struck up a conversation, gave her the card, and she admitted she was married. I immediately asked her about the blonde lady she was with in the café. She looked put off that I asked about her friend, but I gave her a card asking if she would give it to the blonde.

I gave out cards to five more ladies and at four o'clock

in the afternoon I was sitting at the library computers with Vishal. He was teasing me for my Valentine's Day antics when Alaina sent me an instant message on the computer. She looked me up on the social network and sent me a picture of the Valentine that her married friend had given her.

I found out she was a natural blonde, was twenty years old, had two dogs, five cats, a few rodents, lived in a house that her father bought her, drove a huge red pickup truck, and her nickname was *Princess*. In the following week, we drank alcohol together on a video call, sent text messages back and forth every day, and spent every bit of time together between classes having coffee and cigarettes in her truck. Meeting Alaina relieved me because I rarely meet women on a romantic level, and I considered the connection to be a small miracle.

My favourite time with her was on a Thursday last month when I read her half of chapter five from Jack Kerouac's novel, *The Dharma Bums*. It's a chapter about a character named Ray Smith and all of his friends having a twenty year old blonde named Princess at their shack in California to experience yabyum, which is described in the book as a kind of sacred Buddhist orgy. I read the chapter to Alaina, including the part where Princess sits her naked body on another naked hipster's lap, the part explaining Smith's reluctance to get naked in a room full of his male peers, and continued reading up until the part where the lead character, Smith, is sitting in a tub with Princess completely naked, making plans to do yabyum every Thursday.

Clean Fill Wanted:

Easy As ____________________________

Until that moment, times with Alaina were rather superficial, but when I surreptitiously showed her that she resembled, almost identically, a character in a book by an author I touted as being one of literature's greatest, I felt as though I had transcended beyond merely being with her. Karl Jaspers, an existentialist philosopher and psychologist who left psychology because it relied on medications that did not work, and the methods of practice, to him, were futile for patients, says that our primary goal as humans is to transcend in some way, and we attempt to transcend by revealing ourselves to others. He also says that we are never able to fully realize if we have transcended because, for the most part, our awareness is only of ourselves.

It was clear that I had connected with Alaina. I knew I had transcended with the reading. "Where do you find this stuff?" Alaina said. In truth, it's a mainstay at your typical public library, but I didn't want to come off as pompous, so I said, "It's my favourite book of all time. I've read it twice," And then she invited me to visit her at her house on the following Thursday night, right after I had my injection at the hospital at the end of February.

So, I arrived at the doctor's office last month, and saw the nurse and doctor. My favourite part is seeing the nurse. I'm in my early thirties and she's older than me, but she's cute and she talks to me like we're friends and it's very candid. She knows I was a musician and one time I described to her the differences between the male and female vocal chords and how their size differences affect our aural perception because males are more inclined to hear and produce lower tones, making the sounds of females more exotic to males. I thought it would be interesting to her because she's in the medical profession.

Because it was the end of the day and my mind was fixated on the idea of spending the night with Alaina, I couldn't focus on anything the nurse was saying. "Why are you acting weird?" she asked. I told her I was going to a woman's house for the first time and I was kind of nervous. I asked the nurse if she would ask me about it at my next visit. "Just be safe and don't do anything that makes you uncomfortable," she said. I got my injection and rushed over to Alaina's house on the bus, in the freezing February weather. The sky was clear and the air was tight.

I was hungry, so when I got off of the bus I went into a convenience store and bought a bag of potato chips with my last two dollars. I had no gloves or hat on and as I walked that last bit of the way to Alaina's house my hands became red, slightly frozen, and lost all agility of my fingers as I ate the chips. I walked right in Alaina's door as she had instructed. She said her dogs would get too excited if I knocked on the door. She also told me to take my shoes off in the bathroom so the dogs didn't eat them or hide them somewhere. As soon as we relaxed on the couch she offered me some potato chips.

My hands warmed up as I rubbed and petted her dogs, letting them lick my hands and face. Alaina and I lay there close together on her couch watching a movie and then some television shows, hardly speaking to one another until around eleven o'clock at night. She told me she wanted to go to bed. I asked her if I should go with her and she said no, so I told her I would leave with just enough time to catch the last bus. I didn't want to wait outside for too long and freeze.

I walked to the bus stop and waited there for a few minutes. I saw one bus pass by on the other side of the road, then my bus came and I got on. I didn't know Alaina's neighbourhood very well, had never been there before, and when I got on the bus, I realized that the first bus I saw was the one I should have taken. It was late and I wasn't sure if I'd be able to get home anymore. Eventually the bus stopped on the far reaches of the city and went out of service. I waited in the cold, direly hoping that a bus might come.

And finally one did. I flashed my bus pass at the driver and he told me it would bring me back across the city to my place. Half-way through the long loop back over to the opposite side of the city, I fell asleep, totally knocked out and my heart sank when I noticed the bus was parked back at the station downtown and I had missed my stop. There were no more busses, and it was a blizzard.

Alaina and I didn't notice that a heavy snowfall had begun while we were together. It wasn't going to let up either, continuing to steadily crescendo as I walked the unplowed downtown streets in the biting February night without gloves or a hat. There were a few pubs open downtown and some of them had live bands inside. The pubs looked so uninviting with the large drifts of snow covering the doorways. I thought of the summer when the doors were always swinging open, and people out on the sidewalks smoking.

I became pensive of the time in my life, almost ten years ago, when I too was a numismatist, peddling pop songs for whatever compensation I could get. I felt alone on the empty streets with the snow whirling into my cold hands and face.

Yet, I became elated with a calm of surrender in realizing the magnificence of how each modular element congealed into transcendental abstraction. I immediately remembered that my disability pension for March was deposited into my bank account at the stroke of midnight that night, so I took a cab home and thought of how I would embellish to the nurse the details of a story that was only dry and exceedingly depressing in the few moments before seeing it all for the beauty of the storm.

The last time I saw the doctor, I was overly anxious about visiting Alaina, with hopes of being close to a woman for the first time in my life, to hail anything transmundane from the experience. This time, the nurse called on me and I followed her into her office. "How have you been?" she asked. I was wondering if she would ask about Alaina as I had instructed her to, at the end of my last visit. To answer her question, I told her I had recently finished reading a book. I pulled the Kerouac book, *Big Sur*, out of my satchel and discussed it with her to seem as though I was avoiding the subject of Alaina. The nurse seemed to enjoy the musings I shared about Kerouac—his way of living and way of writing. I told her Kerouac was once on *The Jack Benny Show* claiming that all of his stories were true. "Oh yeah?" she asked sort of interestedly, "I know of that show, it was before my time though." I told her Kerouac read an excerpt of On the Road while Benny played some jazz on the piano. "But yeah, it's more my dad's time," I said

And finally she asked me about Alaina—she's such a curious nurse. I experienced a frenzy of excitement as I was about to recount my experience. I didn't want to let her know that my time with Alaina, sitting on the couch and watching television, was antithetical to my ideals. At the psychiatrist's office, everything in my life is perfect, any slight discourse a cause for alarm and arduous consequences, so I improvised a lacunal story involving only the seductive spirit of our closeness on the couch and how I returned home in a lovely haze, still bewildered by the magic of being with Alaina. Heck, in actuality, the story I gave the nurse was completely true, leaving out only the part about the zoological miasma. Then the nurse gave me my injection.

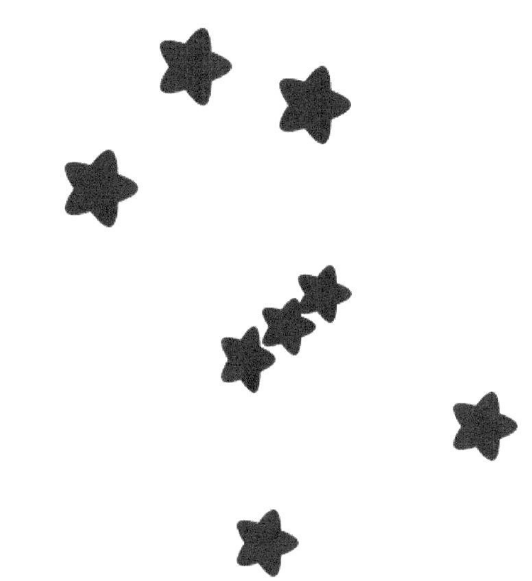

Orion

POETRY

I went to sleep
early tonight
to wake up
before the morning
to see Orion
over the park
imagining a place
where nothingness
is inconsequential
of your absence

J. Dewanstra

TO THE CALVIN KLEIN MOM JEANS AT GOODWILL

In the beginning you stayed white and fair
And often forgiving as well
When in the wash with pink underwear
Never a complaint did you sell

Though from goodwill I found you
I see your pockets in jeans I pass by
And since I spilled tequila on you
Whenever I see mom jeans I cry

Shall I complain because you're ruined?
Or blame myself for the incident?
Your button torn and seams loosened
No longer pristine, but still magnificent

Yet I'm hopeful this stain may fade,
Let it be known on my legs you've laid.

Kate Blackwood

Abraham Dozing in a Café on a Snowy Morning

Michael Whone

Aliens?
Claims of NASA dissidents;
Dissenters of publics
Seeking Magicks.

Double your sun, double your pleasure!
Retrograde evolutionary mishap
As fodder less science than fiction;
Less magic than Isaac.

Enchanted—
The insidious hordes'
Lapses of peripeteia
—so as not to awaken

From smokescreen to poetry;
The despair leaving adolescence.
The truth is not found
In spaces that had us lain

With regret, surmising
Nothing on ourselves.
Awaken,
Ethereal flake, creasing

To nourish, to show
The vagrant moments,
Life's Beatific rivulets,
But not

To specious revelations (Settling
in reels' Alpha males
& sluts
Fell colossal heels

On Snowflakes
Or lyrical subtleties of brooks)
Babbling Tinseltown-Godhead
Magic.

Adaptation 2019

CORY VDV

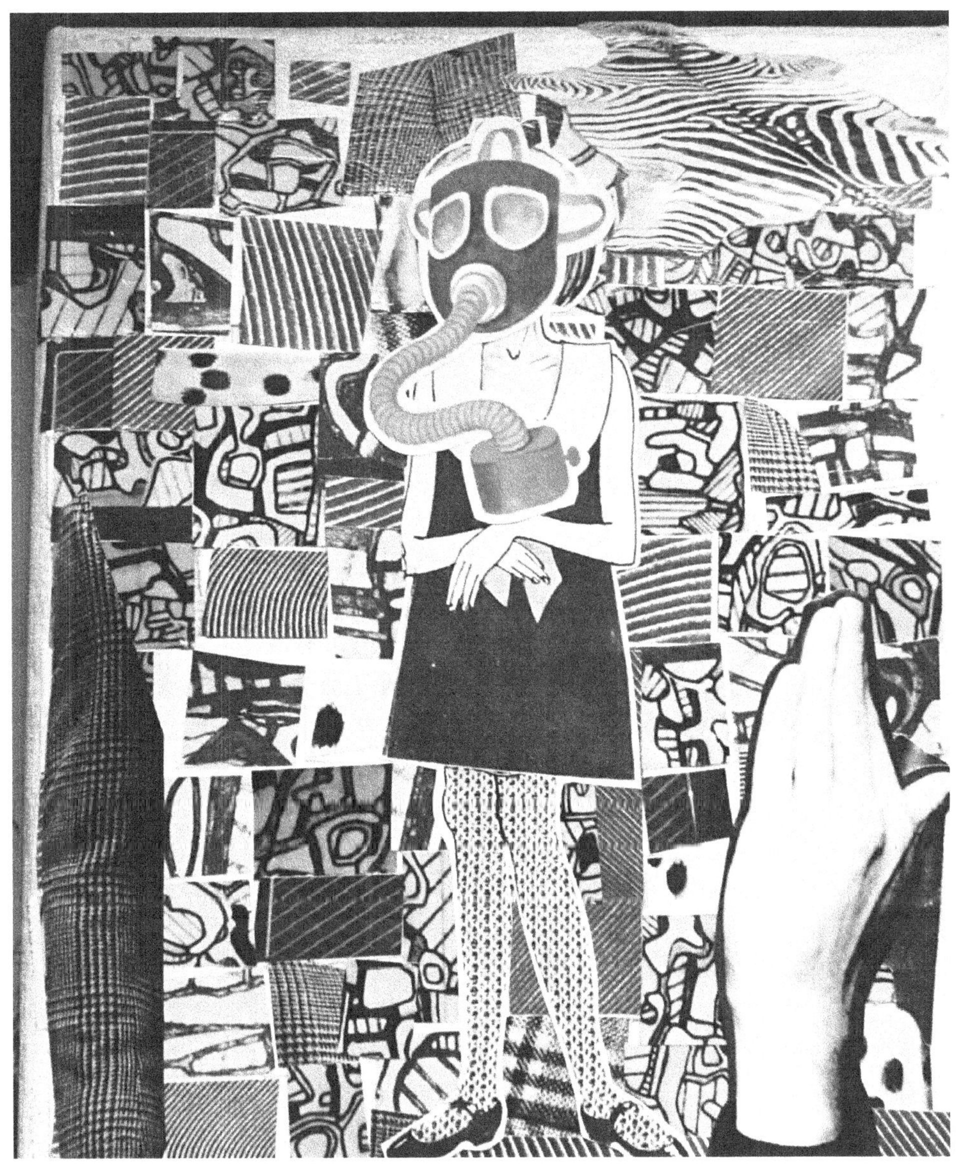

Mixed Media

The Day Willow Went

Linda Laforge

0:15 | 02.06.2105

Mina repeatedly scrutinized the surveillance monitors of her lab to find some clue to how her identical sister could have disappeared. Nothing would have said fatherly love like state-of-the-art equipment from their adopted father and Con Corp's CEO, specially given the importance of their research. It was only one of the three largest multi-national conglomerates in the world—among their enterprises, the manufacture of computers, phones and tablets, an online banking platform and credit division. Even with the antiquated video, it was clear enough for her to see everything from multiple angles.

She and her sister looked entirely alike. Mirror twins, with warm olive skin, sharp blue eyes and cropped jet black hair. She could certainly observe why the lab team nicknamed them El Chapo. It wasn't just for their heritage, lack of height and stocky build. Her own need for control over all aspects was certainly part of it. They were exactly the same in look, sound and movement. Not the archetypal nerds in lab coats they watched growing up and not who *Popular Science* want on their cover.

Willow was laughing and celebrating with the team.

Bev, the team bio-engineer, entered the lab with the results. She vibrated with excitement. William, their lab grunt, fell asleep face down at his station.

That's when I stepped in. I'd let it go on for much too long. I wasn't planning on giving up.

She must have watched the video thirty times before she saw it. She'd gone through every computer and every memory module in the lab that covered a span of two months. She'd postulated many theories. She thought she might have sent Willow into some other dimension or stranded her in some unknown coordinates, or she could even be trapped in a random quantum void. Realistically, none of that was possible. How could she see this now? Had her mind filled this in to fit some narrative she made up to make her feel better? To keep functioning? No. That couldn't be. She had to be too tired and stressed to think straight.

I did keep trying. I never gave up.

"Sleep," I whispered. "You can sleep now. The project is a success."

She heard me, through all of the clutter in her incredibly active brain. I fought all the garbage in her head. Mina curled up under her workstation on the cement floor in the lab, her arms wrapped around the warm fleshy memory center she created and closed her eyes. She slept fully and deeply, for the first time in years. Fifteen years, to be precise.

Mina went to her office, which doubled as her home and climbed to the top bunk. The bottom bunk of her childhood bed was piled with books on quantum physics, bio-chemistry and project notes, along with a scattering of empty ketchup chip bags and Willow's frilly blouses and gaudy dresses ablaze with every colour under the sun. She shared this room with Willow. The smell of her brought tears to her dry, tired eyes.

Dropping quickly down from the bunk and out the door, she ran the hall until she exhausted all of her already limited energy. It wasn't far. She wasn't one to move much. She took a few deep breaths and found herself at her workstation.

She slept for three days.

Her team was ordered to stay away.

"My God, it's about time," said her adopted father Archibald, President of Con Corp, from his office on the top floor of the 100 storey complex, as he watched her on his shiny new 3D monitor.

I spoke to her as she slept. I whispered all the things she needed to know straight into her mind. I told her how to find me.

04:05 | 12.18.2104

Everyone in the lab was silent as they listened to the equipment slowly surge. Their eyes were glued to Chamber A, a closed seven foot tall ringed metallic cylinder. The chambers were sectioned off by UV coated windows to protect their eyes. The team watched a close-up of the organic carrot through their own flat monitors, in its clear glass pot where they could see its roots reach for nourishment. Various coloured lasers beamed the carrot from all sides to collect every tiny nuance of it, from its DNA to its bioactive compounds.

"Donut is a go," William announced as the fat white MRI started down around the glass tube to scan the subject and build a detailed spatial image. It caused minor video interference, making the monitors sketchy while it riffed along. Everyone relaxed in their seats. It was the slowest part of the process.

After ten minutes, the data of the completed scan was on its way to the computer. The little carrot was still in the giant glass chamber.

Willow's supercomputer buzzed and beamed away as it received millions of gigaquads of information. It was nothing like the noises their antiquated childhood computer made when it ticked or when the fan kicked in.

This sound was different. Willow's creation was breathing, gurgling and hissing. Mina's twin glared into the data streams, as a rough but fully dimensional sketch of the carrot appeared before her, line by line. She stretched her thumb and forefinger apart in the light of the image to increase the view of the bluish looking root vegetable through her holographic monitor. The crude display lit her from below, making Mina giggle at her evil looking sister. Willow paid no attention, occupied with her computer's bio-electric nano systems as though she herself were coursing through its veins. The whirring, although not loud, increased in pace as the system received the mapping information of the organic carrot. Suddenly there was real silence. The carrot was in the machine. At least its molecular data was. The first portion of this experiment was complete.

"Hit it, Willow," Mina blurted. Her sister ignored her and kept looking over the data. "Go on!"

"I'm checking everything first, Mina," she said quietly as she eyed every detail of the report on her monitor.

"This would've been easier if I had time for my upgrade."

"Slowing down the project for two months to install another of your unstable and untested gadgets ... I mean, really!" Mina tried to focus.

"Whatever." Willow hit the continue button on her floating monitor. "Let's go, baby. Show El Chapo what you can do."

Her white fleshy computer began pulsing and whirring softly for several minutes as the team waited in stiffened anticipation for the rest of this massive data stream to travel from the fastest computer in the world to Chamber B. They'd tested different plant life, mostly simple root veggies, over 100 times. Although they may have either killed or spliced some bizarre and frightening looking new species in the process, only the last six were completely successful. The tension in the room was arresting.

"The egg is loaded," Bev reported.

It had been aptly named for its shape. Chamber B was an eight feet high, almost six feet in circumference, titanium contraption. It had its own noises that were akin to sitting beside someone in an outhouse in both sound and smell. It needed the right temperature, humidity and material to do its job.

After seven minutes, Chamber B held an exact duplicate of the organic carrot, intact, in the same clear pot.

The lab erupted into thunderous applause. That is, everyone but Mina. Willow appeared elated to see that this time the computer did its job point zero zero two percent more efficient than last time. It was the only computer in the world fast enough and big enough to make her twin's theory a reality. Willow was frozen by her overwhelming feelings of relief and immense pride in her sister.

"Not so fast," Mina yelled, her hands in the air to shush everyone.

Bev jumped to her feet and ran to Chamber B. She stood before the slightly open hatch of the steaming chamber and took in a big breath before pulling it fully open and going in.

“How’s it look?” Mina was still frozen to her seat. She needed this to work. She had less than ten hours before their demo to the Con Corp execs. She’d been at *Project Scotty* since she graduated from Cal Tech with her PhD in physics. Her parents died just a few years before that. She was only twelve when Archibald came to save the day. A few years after that Willow earned her second degree in genetics and moved into the lab. She felt like she had claimed someone else’s life, someone else’s memory, so disconnected from everything before she began *Project Scotty*. It was better that way. She didn’t have to remember arid Mapimî, Mexico. She didn’t have to think about the twinkle in her mother’s tired eyes or her dirty hands from working the fields. Thinking of her exhausted father when he came home from the mines at night, unable to stand straight anymore, made her feel empty in her core. Her tunnel vision allowed her to do nothing but *Project Scotty*, unless it was something that would propel it along. Everyone, including her parents, her rich adopted father, expected many things from her. She was supposed to have changed the world by the time she was twenty. She was almost thirty-three.

“Bev!”

Bev knelt over the little carrot, scanning it with her sleek white mobile laser scanner. “Well,” she yelled out the door, “so far it looks pretty much like a carrot.” Glancing out the big door at William, her pursed lips twisted into a smirk. “Are you getting this data?”

“Yes, Ma’am. It looks like a carrot from here too.” He smiled, raising his thick unibrow high in glee. “No degradation at all. It's looking pretty, well, alive!" A few cheers exploded from the team. He nodded and laughed.

"Just a few more scans and I'll get it into the lab and take a detailed look."

"It's not degrading? Not at all?" Mina asked, body stiff at the thought.

"Mina!" Willow barked. "What's with you? It worked, successfully, six times before. Why do you always have to rain on everyone's parade? We did it! You did it! Let's break out the champagne!"

The whole team looked at Willow. Until she completed her bio computer system, also a work far ahead of its time, few in the scientific community took either of them seriously.

She knew they looked the same, but it felt like only she understood how different they were. Mina watched as her twin became more relaxed and social once she completed the first prototype of her incredibly unique computer, which merged both metal and biological material to handle large speed-of-light data streams. It wasn't just a Quantum computer. It was something no one had ever thought up before. It used fungal material she engineered to specifically act as a conduit, allowing data streams to travel faster than the human brain. She would brag to high heaven how brilliant she was to design an intelligent mycelial network that 'talked' tech through a computer rather than to trees. Willow reached her goal of creating this, her first product of genius, when she was twenty. That was thirteen years ago.

Mina wasn't even close. Thirteen years ago, *Science*

Magazine predicted Mina's theories wouldn't be proven for generations to come, if ever. So, while Willow basked in the glory and the profits of her continued success, Mina was bitter. She determined that *Project Scotty* would outdo her twin. Finally.

Now, after twenty-one years of working through the night, primarily alone, the Biological Duplication theory wasn't only proven. She had built the machine that made it happen. And it worked. It could change the world in immeasurable ways. And she didn't know how to feel. She wanted this to belong to her and only her. Mina knew she'd end up sharing credit with her sister. It wouldn't have happened without her stupid computer. A twinge of guilt flushed her face red.

Bev ran off to the conservatory with the new carrot. Her job had just begun and it was already 2 a.m. Willow had broken open the bubbly, ecstatic. Mina knew both of them should stand tall. They could shove all those doubts and insults down the throats of those egomaniacal bastards in the scientific community who put them up as nothing more than sci-fi fanatics.

She took a swig of champagne from the bottle with a reluctant smirk. The others laughed and shouted and cheered. She smiled as she looked at her sister, grabbed the bottle from William and chugged some down, spilling it all over her face and neck. Willow always threw it in her face that she was older by five minutes. It would have been so much easier if someone else had a computer big enough for the job.

"Are you OK Mina? Why are you looking at me like that?"

Willow put her glass down.

"This one is mine. Sure, you helped with your computer, but I did this," Mina said in a low monotone voice, narrowing her eyes. "I did this. I am not sharing this one with you. You have no right to the spotlight on this one!"

Willow stood back in awe. "Mina? What the hell?"

Mina took the champagne bottle and walked away.

10:05 | 12.19.2104

Mina went to her office, grabbed some ketchup chips from an open bag and climbed up to the top bunk. The chips were stale. She looked down at the classic books piled on the bottom bunk. *The Age of Entanglement* by Louisa Gilder. She felt forever entangled with her sister. Why did she feel so angry? So jealous? *The Ghost in the Atom* by Davies and Brown was tattered and worn. She felt haunted by her mixed emotions. *How to Teach Physics to Your Dog* by Orzel. Mina laughed. That was her sister's book. She swung her feet from the bunk, took a few deep breaths and thought about laying down. She was tired. She never slept anymore.

Everyone was still at work when she returned for the big project presentation for Con Corp's heads. Energy was high, even though no one had slept a wink.

"Somebody check that the cameras are running?" Willow

belted out. "Oh! Hey El Chapo. Hope you got a cat nap in."

"I did," Mina lied as she put her coffee down beside her soon to be obsolete keyboard. "Don't start with the El Chapo stuff. You know I hate it." She turned to the crew. "So, are the cameras rolling?"

"Yes, the cameras are all on and working." William smiled. It was annoying how he always smiled. "They've been recording since last night's test. You want me to go get the next test subject from the conservatory?"

"Yeah. Get moving, guys. We've got a show to put on." Bev appeared tired at her station as she set up her system. "Bev! Nice reporting on the carrot. That's gonna look great to the suits."

"Oh?" She looked surprised at Mina. "Thanks. I know you like to be thorough."

"What, no apologies?" Willow scoffed as she focused her eyes on her 3D monitor.

"For what? Protecting my own interests?" Mina retorted. "I was just making it clear whose project this is."
"Whatever." Willow shook her head. "I'm disappointed in you, Mina. You're such an ass at times."

With the exception of the added tension between the twins, everything was perfect when the suits entered the lair, a 15,000 square foot lab deep underground. The old boys, and two women, got off the elevator laughing like a handful of fat old college chums. You could still see it in their demeanor as they stood there, a level above, looking down at the team from the observation room through protective glass. They had made a big investment in Mina and were eager to get a glimpse at what their return was going to look like. She didn't care about that, she thought, as she looked up at her father as he winked at her. He wasn't much like a dad, but he was all she had. It was beautiful. A big fat radish disappeared in a flash. The suits smiled and applauded. Willow's super-computer whizzed and purred until it had the radish from Chamber A in its servo-molecular grips. It sent the information to Chamber B in another brilliant flash. You could feel the excitement build as they all listened to the machine sing in anticipation of the appearance of a shiny new duplicate. Then came the second flash. There it was. One new radish in Chamber B. Two radishes for the price of God-only-knows. The suits clapped and cheered. Mina was finally smiling. She'd done it and she'd impressed them. The pressure should have been off.

Mina looked over to Willow's station. She was gone. She should have been over there 'hoop-hooing' and shouting something annoying. Bev, avoiding Mina's gaze, had already run over to the second chamber to scan the radish. William was scrutinizing the new data as he received it, meticulous as always. But Willow wasn't there. "How could she leave at a time like this?" Mina thought. "She's not the jealous one. And she doesn't usually walk out when she's pissed off. I'm the one who does that. And there was a crowd to perform for."

14:35 | 12.19.2104

Mina could only theorize, after reviewing the video of the last thirty-six hours. No one had left the lab in more than a week. In less than one one thousandth of a second, Willow had vanished, and in precisely the same flash that brought the radish to Chamber B. She saw Bev at her station. William at his. She saw herself at her own. Willow was gone from hers. She just couldn't see what happened. Bev and William did look away from their work to her, offering each other quizzical expressions. Were they in on something?

9:15 | 02.06.2105

"But it worked flawlessly six times before we presented the Molecular Replicator to the Board. It can't be shut down!" Mina paced. She was wearing an old pair of jeans and a ragged, food stained t-shirt with Rocket Raccoon almost worn off.

"We're not shutting it down. We're removing you from the project. " Uncle Archibald never seemed to understand his daughter, or was he just President Conwell now, and she just his disappointing prize scientist?

"But it's *my* project! No one else can continue it. No one! Why would you take it away from me?"

"Because your sister is dead," he said sharply.

"Nobody knows that!"

Archibald got up from behind his immense old mahogany desk, buttoned his navy suit coat over his rotund belly and walked towards his office doors. "You haven't made any progress retrieving your sister from wherever it is you sent her, and considering you have continually refused to see a reputable psychiatrist since we began working together oh so many years ago, I have no choice. You're off the project." He walked her towards the door.

"Since we began working together?" She briskly wiped away the tear as it welled up in her eye. "I guess we were never family, were we."

"You never leave your dungeon, my dear."

"This is my whole life. You have to give me more time!"

"You've had two months since she's disappeared and all you talk about is the project." He put his hands on her shoulders and looked directly into her eyes. "Where's your sister?"

Mina's eyes filled with tears. Everything was being taken away from her. Everything. She held her weary head high as she pushed away from him, knowing that twenty-one years of her life were being flushed down a toilet. She had no idea where she would go, except to follow the walls down the long hall, passed by busy suits doing busy things.

~ ~ ~ ~

"She's a mess," the suit laughed as he walked by the company's mysterious star, towards his figurehead. "I saw the whole conversation from the boardroom."

"Yes, she's a mess." They walked back into his spacious office. "She's done it. She's actually done it and no one ever believed it was possible."

"You did!" the fat white man let out a low deep belly laugh. "You did. We're going to rule the world, my friend. Rule the world."

"I know. We can duplicate living matter! And we thought the bio computer was big. Not that we know what to do with it large scale yet. Kinda freaks people out." Archibald Conwell waved his hand in just such a way that a snappy hidden bar silently rolled out of the wall. "But her! Who's in control of the food system now?" He laughed heartily. "All the Agrochemical corporations will be shitting themselves."

The suit and Chief Accounting Officer poured an organic rye and ginger as he laughed, imagining their profits leaping as high as the global temperature graph explaining climate change. He wiped his brow with his satin hanky as his heart rate rose. He took a sip and then felt a pang. "Don't you feel just a little bit guilty over her?"
"No. I don't. She's a lunatic." He plopped a fresh olive in his large martini.

"But she has a lot more ahead of her. She's only in her thirties. Why risk losing her?" He drank back his rye in one gulp. "Her parents made you her legal guardian for a reason, did they not? At least she's safe down there in her dungeon. Isn't she?"

"Don't worry. She'll be fine. She never leaves." He laughed. "I didn't know you were such a softy. She'll go right back down to her lab, and if the company psychologists are correct, she may come back to her senses. I was advised to give her a little push."

"That wasn't a little push, that was a big knock down shove out the door." He poured another rye, this time a double on the rocks.

"Who really cares? Most of the greatest scientists and inventors in history have had a few sparks of brilliance early in their careers. After that they seem to jump in the spotlight and join the mediocre."

"So you don't expect much more from her?" He rolled the icy drink in his hand.

"We've got some new blood coming on board. And the new kid!" He sat in a big chair overlooking his bustling creative complex, several smaller office buildings bright and curvy in design.

"That bright little dude we weeded out a few years ago from the Phillippines?"

"He's just like her."

"Wow," he said, unbuttoning his suit jacket to sit. "I think our current star is different. She could have more for us. If anything, improvements on what she's started."

"You only softy," he laughed and slapped the man's leg. "She's constantly monitored. My little dream girl won't be going anywhere. And she'll be just fine."

10:15 | 02.06.2105

She slept. For three days.

"My God, it's about time," her uncle said, in his office on the hundredth floor, as he watched her on his monitor.

I spoke to her as she slept. I whispered, "There is only one. There is only one, Willomina Conwell," I continued softly, until I was sure she understood.

She awoke saying, "Willomina Conwell? Willow. Mina. Willowmina?"

She rubbed her eyes, sat up amongst the rubble of the first bunk that represented her life. Last she recalled, she was at her work station. Instead, she found herself under the covers of tattered science books and junk food wrappers from the vending machines provided by her adopted father. The CEO. Cement walls, warn carpeted floors and no windows to the outside world.

"Willomina Conwell?" she said again to herself. She cried. She craved a window, vast blue skies, and the endless desert. This would be where to find herself. Her whole self.

The Eternal Dance

POETRY

I have given it much thought.
There seems to be
only one explaination
for why we are here.
Why our souls choose
to incarnate as mortals
only to suffer for a hundred years
over and over again.
I now understand
we were once angels
who chose to manifest as humans
in order to experience the imperfect
and tempestuous human love.
So you see, if angels couldn't refuse love
then who am I to refuse you?
And so, I yeild.
I surrender to this.
Our eternal dance.

River Van Style Review
3/20 Bolero Bird

www.ingramcontent.com/pod-product-compliance
Lightning Source LLC
Chambersburg PA
CBHW080333030726
47593CB00010B/2996

* 9 7 8 1 7 7 5 3 3 0 0 4 2 *